THERE'S HOPE

Breaking Invisible Chains

Presented by
Liz Hoop

Copyright © 2021 Liz Hoop
Publishing services provided by

DWilson & Associates, LLC

All rights reserved. Printed in the United States of America.
No part of this book may be used or reproduced in any manner whatsoever without written permission from the author.

ISBN: 979-8-9852240-0-9

CONTENTS

FOREWORD
Rev. Gary Wilkerson i

INTRODUCTION
My Why 1
Liz Hoop, Project Visionary

CHAPTER 1   *God Won Me Back* 3
            Sarah Kelley

CHAPTER 2   *Unmasking the Truth* 7
            Angel Austin

CHAPTER 3   *It Doesn't Have to Be This Way* 11
            Megan Eakin

CHAPTER 4   *Out of the Darkness Into the Light* 15
            Missy Holland

CHAPTER 5   *From Death to Life* 19
            Lauren Goar

CHAPTER 6   *Raised to Life by Jesus Christ* 23
            Rachel Byrd

CHAPTER 7   *Rise Above!* 25
            Ashley Wise

CHAPTER 8   *Dry Bones Come to Life* 27
            Angie Little

CHAPTER 9   *Bound by Anger Set Free by Jesus Christ* 29
            Randi Jones

CHAPTER 10 *Wrong Choices Righted by Redemption* 31
    Jennifer Ford

CHAPTER 11 *Let Freedom Ring* 35
    Shannon Boose

CHAPTER 12 *From Broken to Conqueror* 41
    Brittany Meeks

CHAPTER 13 *You're Not Good Enough — The Lie I Believed* 43
    Hannah Singletary

CHAPTER 14 *Why Would God Allow Me to Hurt Like This if He Loves Me So Much?* 47
    Shelia Patterson

CHAPTER 15 *From Overdose to Overcomer* 51
    Holley Henderson

CHAPTER 16 *From Rejected to Accepted* 53
    Beth Burgess

CHAPTER 17 *You're Never Too Far Gone* 57
    Tina Von Seutter

CHAPTER 18 *From Death to Beyond Blessed* 59
    Jordan Murphy

CHAPTER 19 *I Found My Voice* 63
    Tiffany Anthony

FOREWORD

By the Rev. Gary Wilkerson
President of World Challenge Inc.

The gospels are full of miraculous stories. They tell of deliverances, healings, salvations, and great signs and wonders. The same power of the Holy Spirit is still at work today. Jesus is still setting captives free, delivering people from bondages, healing the sick, and working miracles. Liz writes passionately about this amazing work of God she has seen. Through the ministry of Adult and Teen Challenge, lives are being transformed, and hope is being restored.

When my father, David Wilkerson, pioneered Teen Challenge more than 60 years ago, he knew in the deepest recesses of his heart something vital: God's power is more than sufficient for any need, crisis, addiction, or family trouble; he knew that nothing is too hard for the Lord. Now, years later, people like Liz continue to believe and know that God can work such miracles.

In the following stories, you will be encouraged, filled with new hope, realize the power of prayer, and see that no matter what you may be facing right now, God has the solution. Reading of the breakthroughs that others have experienced helps those of us who continue to believe and pray for the hurting people we love. For those struggling with addictions and life-controlling problems, these stories offer us a glimpse of what God can do; if He can do it for the folks we read about here, He can do it for us.

The great missionary William Carey said that we should "expect great things from God and attempt great things for God." The book you have in your hand was born out of great expectation and great attempts; as a result, great things have come about.

Gary Wilkerson is an author, public speaker, and the president of World Challenge Inc., an international ministry organization founded by his father, David Wilkerson. He has traveled to speak at mission leadership conferences in 70 different countries and supported church planting, relief, and evangelism among some of the most unreached people groups on earth.

A CrossFit enthusiast, Gary often hikes the Rocky Mountains' breathtaking front range in Colorado. He and his wife, Kelly, live in Colorado Springs with their four children and nine grandchildren.

THERE'S HOPE

FOUNDING SUPPORTERS

Thank you for your support

Dwayne & Deb Robbins
Darrell & Sharon Worley
Debbie Helton
Mary Grantham
Magnolia Springs Assembly of God Church
Cornerstone Church
Dorothy P. Wilson
Northside Assembly of God Church
Three Rivers Assembly of God Church
Sheila Farr
Serene Dumas Lee
Melinda Bowman
LuAnn Pappas
Mike & Terrie McLeod

INTRODUCTION

My Why

By Liz Hoop
Project Visionary

If this time last year, someone had told me I'd be a best-selling author with five different anthology book projects, I would have laughed. But God! He had a plan and a reason for the journey He had started me on. One Sunday evening recently I had been with the women from the Adult and Teen Challenge Center for Women in Poplarville, Miss. As I was driving home from that time with the women, I heard God say to me, "You know all that writing I've had you doing? Now it's time for you to be a visionary author and do it for Adult and Teen Challenge for Women of Mississippi."

I've served on the Board of Directors for several years now for this center. I've seen many women come through those doors — broken, lost, hurt, nobody to show them love, and I've seen the transformations that have occurred in these women. I've seen beauty from ashes and the hope that has been born in them.

My heart jumps for joy every time I listen to their stories and how they've been able to overcome the things that had them in the destructive lifestyle that brought them in and how some have been restored with their families. No one is ever too far gone that God can't restore them.

A woman who graduated from the program several years ago recently said to me, "I wish I would have had this book to read when I first went into the program because I would've been able to see that there was hope for me and what I can expect that God can do for me." That young woman graduated from the program, worked at the center for a while, and is now serving in a ministry. This book will become a part of the curriculum for the program.

My vision for this book is that the one reading it will be able to relate to at least one of the stories and knows a woman who needs this program.

Thank you to all the women who shared their stories and to our supporters who came alongside them to support them to get their stories heard and to help someone else find There's Hope Breaking Invisible Chains.

It has been said that wisdom grows from places of great adversity. Helping others find their way out is philanthropic liaison Liz Hoop, who is a leader, motivator, and servant.

Liz is a multi-time international best-selling author, speaker, and communal leader. She upholds the highest professional standards and describes her trademark as her ability to work well with people from all walks of life. She has many years of experience in marketing and management at the executive level, attributing her success to making people the center of her ethics values. She is the CFO/director of outreach for Anchored Heart Community Resources and serves on the board of directors for the Mental Health Association of South Mississippi, Adopt A Grandparent Day, and Teen Challenge for Women in Mississippi – each role echoing her heart's desire to serve humanity. She is also an active servant in her local faith-based community, where she as a choir member and is a leader of the women's ministry at Magnolia Springs in Hurley, Mississippi.

When Liz is not out volunteering throughout her local community, she enjoys serving others and spending time with loved ones and close friends.

CHAPTER 1

God Won Me Back

By Sarah Kelley

I was raised Catholic and in a very normal family. Both my mom and dad worked to support our family, me being the youngest of my three siblings. On the weekends the adults would have fish fries and crab boils, etc., and the kids would play outside like normal kids do. Every summer, all of the gang would pack up and go on vacation, mostly to Gulf Shores, Ala., and we all had fun.

We would go over to my parents' friends' house, and I would play with my friend. She had a brother who would tell us to play hide and seek. He told us, "I'll hide one of you, and the other will go and find you," but it always took longer to hide me because he would take advantage of me. When he finally let me go, he would tell me I could not say anything because everyone would think I was a very bad girl. He would let me go and move on to my friend, and this went on for a long time. I hated going over there, but I was scared to say anything, so I kept going when my parents went.

I kept this a secret until I got married. In junior high, I started smoking cigarettes and pot with kids around the neighborhood who were all older than I was. In the 10th grade I met the man of my dreams, or so I thought. He introduced me to heavier drugs, but it wasn't until my senior year when my dad passed away that this guy introduced me to the needle. It wasn't the feeling of the drugs I liked anymore; I loved the rush the needle gave me. I married this man, and we had two beautiful girls. We seemed like a normal family on the outside, but in reality, we were functional junkies. I became a people pleaser and worked very hard at pleasing my husband. People pleasing became a second job to me, losing who I was and becoming whoever others needed me to be. We separated, and the kids and I went to stay with my mom. In the meantime, I found out my husband had slept with another woman, and that felt like a knife in my back.

We decided to try to work things out but realized drugs were the only thing we had in common in the nine and a half years we were married, so we divorced. A guy I knew introduced me to crack cocaine. Crack took me further than I ever wanted to go, kept me there longer than I wanted to stay, and cost me a lot more than I ever wanted to pay. I became homeless and hopeless real fast. My oldest daughter became pregnant with my first grandchild, and I kept telling myself I didn't want to be a grandma who smoked crack. The day my granddaughter was born, she was so beautiful and perfect, but my trying to be a grandma who didn't smoke crack was a short-lived effort.

After enduring many abusive relationships, being homeless, going repeatedly to jail, and never seeing my family, I knew something had to change — plus, I was nearing 50 years old. I saw some people I knew, and they said, "Come go to church with us, and on Monday we will take you to the Stephens Center to fill out an application," so I went to church with them. I ended up getting arrested that night. Going to jail was different this time; I dedicated my life to Christ, and the month I was in there something began happening on the inside of me.

The judge said I could go to rehab, but I would have to find one soon — before the day my 11-year sentence would start at Rankin County Prison. I didn't understand it at the time, but I had this peace that I would find a place. One day before my sentence was to start, a bed became available at Teen Challenge of Mississippi. He's an on-time God!

I entered Teen Challenge October 25, 2012. I learned how to have a personal relationship with the Lord, which filled the emptiness I'd been trying to fill with drugs and men. The Lord's grace, His Word, and the people He used as a vessel at T.C. started chipping away at my guilt and shame, healing my wounds and making me whole after 35 years of being a drug addict. He also began restoring my family back to me.

My stand-on verse while I was at Teen Challenge was Hebrews 12:2 *"Keep your eyes on Jesus for He first began and finished this race we're in. Study how He did it because He never lost sight of where He was going."*

I completed Teen Challenge in 2014, moved back to Pascagoula and did well for three years. I got my own place to live, and old friends started coming back around. I started dabbling in the drugs again, which in turn led to my stealing from my daughter. I guess you could say I took my eyes off of Jesus and gave the enemy a foothold. My daughter had me thrown in jail, and in reality, she really saved my life, because that's when the drug of my choice — opioids — I could no longer get. I was an IV user, and that could have very well been the death of me. A very special woman from Teen Challenge got me from jail, and I was blessed to be able to return to Teen Challenge as a restoration student. The Lord gave me a stand-on verse as soon as I was able to open my Bible: Hosea 2:14-15, which says, *"But then I will win her back once again. I will lead her into the desert and speak tenderly to her there. I will return her vineyards to her and transform the Valley of Trouble into her Gateway of Hope."*

Since being at Teen Challenge the second time, I understand why He gave me that stand-on verse. He has definitely won me back! I'm on staff now at the center, and I oversee the kitchen, but trust me, I'm in love with my Lord and Savior like I've never been before. So, He allows me to do much more than just oversee the kitchen. I am privileged and blessed to help other women who are just like I was — broken, lost and abused. I get to introduce them to a man who will never leave them, who will love them no matter what they've done. His name is Jesus Christ! I get to be part of showing these ladies what it feels like to be loved without wanting anything in return. To see brokenness come through the doors and watch a person's countenance turn to beauty, that is a blessing from the God I serve. Like Colossians 3:23 says, *"Whatever you do, work at it with all your heart, as working for the Lord, not for humans."*

So, my job at Teen Challenge is a blessing, and as long as the Lord allows me, I will keep blessing it forward.

CHAPTER 2

Unmasking The Truth

By Angel Austin

Living a double life does things to a person. It forces you to adapt quickly to even the worst circumstances. It teaches you how to hide behind masks. It creates within you an unquenchable desire to please people at all costs, and it buries any resemblance of your true self deep beneath all the manufactured and rehearsed versions you have so carefully displayed.

Most of my life has been framed this way — chaos and confusion where nobody could see and a huge smile with a side of perfectionism where they could.

Innocence goes out the window when your father is an alcoholic/addict. I saw and experienced things that no child ever should. There were no rules, and there were always less-than-upstanding people around the house. My brother and I stayed with Daddy every other weekend. Our saving grace during those years was my sweet Granny, who would often come pick us up to stay with her. My daddy loved us as much as someone devoured by sin can love another person. When I was at my mama's and pop's house, life was extremely different. Rules were strict, and Mama and Pop expected excellence and obedience. Those are not bad things to expect, but for a child in the emotional and mental state I was in, it seemed like the opposite of love. I know now that they just wanted me to do my absolute best, but I thought it meant my best wasn't good enough. I always felt torn between two different lives — two different versions of myself. I constantly compared myself to my brother and sister, and I always concluded that I fell short.

It became second nature for me to do whatever it took to make people proud of me. If I could just be the best at everything I did, people would approve of me. If I could always be happy and kind, people would accept me. If I loved others until it hurt, people would love me. If I could just pretend that I was okay even when I wasn't, one day I would be.

Unable to reconcile all the turmoil inside me, I started running away from everything that was uncomfortable, pushing my family away. I moved out, and since my parents had instilled an excellent work ethic in me, I did well for an 18-year-old on her own. Working hard, I supported myself, getting into college on an academic scholarship. During this time, my daddy had a massive stroke that paralyzed him, and he moved into a nursing home. He was angry, and so was I — angry and hurt.

I got married during nursing school, and a couple years later, we started our family. We had two beautiful sons, a home, careers, and what appeared to be a perfect little life. It wasn't. After I'd lived so many years of ups and downs, the facade began to crumble away. I was broken and defeated by my own unmet expectations. Single motherhood was hard, and I was so stubborn, insecure, and prideful that I wouldn't ask for help. I was determined to prove I could do it on my own. I couldn't. Meanwhile, my failures and flaws ate at me, leaving my babies with a shell of the mother I desired to be.

I married again, only to realize that I had brought my old issues into a new relationship. Then my daddy died, causing more upset. Between my need to be needed and all the problems we both had, my second marriage ended abruptly.

I had been emotionally bankrupted. All illusion of control and sound judgment was lost. I sought affection wherever I could get it and spiraled down into darkness. Unable to care for my children anymore, I was empty and desperate. One wrong person on one bad day in one weak moment slipped me into a nearly four-year methamphetamine addiction. Suffering emotional, mental, verbal, sexual, and physical abuse by people who said they loved me had stripped me of my dignity, security, and sanity. I developed chemical dependency quickly, and what started out as a way to stay awake longer and numb my broken heart became a runaway train headed straight toward my grave. I couldn't function without it. My health and life were at risk daily. I had become the very thing I swore I would never be. I wanted to do right and get my boys back so we could be a family again like they deserved, but every time I thought about them or anything good, I would hear, "They'd be better off without you." That voice —- those voices of the enemy — tormented me day and night. I was losing my mind, and suicide seemed to be my only way out. I was hospitalized, sent to a critical care unit, and went to a mental health clinic and a rehab facility. Nothing helped. I got clean for a few months, but the underlying issues weren't being addressed, and I took a nose-dive back into addiction and utter hopelessness.

Had my family not sent me to Teen Challenge, I would be dead today. God delivered me from addiction, depression, anxiety, and mental illness at Teen

Challenge. I have been saved and set free by Jesus, and John 8:36 says that *when He sets you free, you will be free indeed!* He has restored my children back to me, too. I graduated from the program in December 2020, and I am currently working here as an intern, helping other ladies develop a relationship with Jesus and turn their lives around. Deuteronomy 31:8 says *"It is the Lord who goes before you. He will be with you; He will never leave you or forsake you. Do not fear or be dismayed."* As I look back at all the times I felt alone, I can clearly see that God was with me through it all. There is hope; His name is Jesus!

CHAPTER 3

It Doesn't Have to Be This Way

By Megan Eakin

In November 2018, I had been at two rehabs in one month, and I found myself at my dealer's house. I got my meth and my needle, and I shot up. I walked to my car, shut the door, and I heard people laughing at me. I turned around, thinking someone was in my car, but to my surprise it was only me in the car. I had no idea that the next four months would be the scariest time of my life, as this overwhelming darkness and the voices followed me everywhere I went, criticizing every single move I made.

I had been using meth since I was 15. I was very insecure, because of abuse and trauma from a young age. When I tried meth for the first time, it made me feel invincible; I felt like I was so strong and confident, and when I was sober, I was very shy and timid. I had no idea it was killing me.

When my mother was pregnant with me, she and my father got a divorce. The enemy used this to warp my mind at a very young age. I believed growing up that every bad thing that happened around me was because of my existence. I knew about God and the devil; I was practically raised in the church when I was a kid. I got baptized at 8 years old, but I had no idea you could have an intimate relationship with Christ.

I am the middle child of three children. Some people call this middle-child syndrome. My sister and brother played sports, and honestly, they were the family favorites. Comparison is a killer. I thought since I wasn't like them, I should be like someone else. So, I chose to go down the path of my dad. He was an alcoholic, and he abused drugs.

That is all I ever knew about him. So, at a young age I started drinking and smoking. I ended up leaving school and getting my GED. I had probably 10 jobs by the time I turned 19. There was just no stability at all in my life.

One day I had been up for days after shooting up crystal meth. I was coming down, and all these emotions came crashing in, and I felt so depressed — the kind of depressed you can't explain. I was in such a dark place. I finally got the courage to contact one of my old friends who had gotten sober. She was the first girl I ever used meth with. Her name is Sarah. She talked me into going to a six-month, faith-based program called The Father's House. After about a month or so of wondering whether I should go, I decided to go. This was one of the lowest points in my life, when my stepdad had tried to abuse me.

I left my family's home, and I was sleeping on someone's floor because I had nowhere to go. I packed some clothes, and I went to that rehab. One night at church I met Jesus, but Satan was after me, I ended up following a girl at the rehab, and we left. Long story short, I tried to come back, and they sent me to another rehab to try to get help.

I was back at my mother's and I couldn't get meth out of my head. I remember clear as day, I was studying my Recovery Bible and just put it down and got into my car and went to get high. After getting high, I started to hear the voices again.

I convinced myself I had just done too many drugs and that I was schizophrenic, I had no idea I was in a spiritual war. When I would shower, the voices would laugh at me and call me names. I would lie in bed at night and see black figures hovering over me. The voices I was hearing were the voices of the people I loved the most. The torment was so bad that I almost killed myself. I would get on the road and walk for miles trying to escape the voices. They wouldn't leave me; I didn't know they were coming from within me.

The only place I felt safe was church. I went to The Ark of Praise, and Pastor Gary Jennings tried to get me to go to Teen Challenge because I had gotten so bad. One day I was sitting outside, and I realized life didn't have to be this way. I now know it was a revelation from God. As tears ran down my face, I finally called Teen Challenge.

The next week was hell trying to get to Teen Challenge. Satan fought me so hard, he put people in my life to keep me from going, but God wanted me there! I had never heard of Teen Challenge, but after Pastor Gary mentioned it, I heard about it on TV, the radio, random people would mention it to me. God was confirming it was where He wanted me.

I walked into Teen Challenge feeling very angry, and I was still hearing the voices tormenting me. Not even a minute after walking into the door, my soul felt peace. I was finally safe. I didn't know it was God's peace. Upon arriving I was in spiritual warfare. The voices were so bad and were trying to tell me everyone there was going to kill me, but every chance I tried to leave, God made it so I couldn't. A week later, I got saved. The voices stopped, and peace flooded my heart, now God started his miraculous work within me.

I was still angry about everything that happened to me. God took my angry heart and flooded it with His joy. He took away my depression and taught me how to work through my feelings. That was one of the biggest things God taught me. He taught me how my feelings are real, but sometimes they aren't valid. He taught me that I can't depend on my feelings, that I can depend on Him and His word.

Teen Challenge taught me how to have healthy relationships, boundaries, and how to walk out my relationship with Jesus Christ. He is my Lord and Savior, and He is all I will ever need.

God gave me the name Jared at Teen Challenge; a year later God confirmed to me I had met Jared. He is now my husband. We were both working at a faith-based facility. Now I am working at a bank where I get to minister to broken souls daily as God leads me too, and Jared works at a rehabilitation center and is a few classes away from getting his social work degree. While God was working on me in Teen Challenge, God was working on Jared at another facility. God's timing is amazing, and He is showing me that daily.

CHAPTER 4

Out of the Darkness into the Light

By Missy Holland

I had a pretty normal life. I was a happy child until I wasn't. Our family moved a lot, and when I was about 10 years old, I began struggling with my weight. I didn't fit in anywhere; I didn't belong. I had a hard time making friends because I was the new fat kid.

When I was 15, our family moved to Memphis, Tenn., and I seemed to settle in. I made friends, got my first job, and did well in school. Once I graduated high school, I did like many other kids do and succumbed to peer pressure.

I started drinking and tried drugs. I met my first husband and had two children, but I started having health problems because of my weight. I tried everything to lose weight and decided to have gastric bypass surgery. When I started losing weight, I started feeling better about myself, but my marriage began to suffer because I was a different person.

I started getting attention from other men and soon started having an affair. This went on a few years until I was sexually assaulted at work. This is when my life truly changed. I began to drink excessively and became addicted to sleeping pills. All I wanted to do was escape the memories and to feel nothing.

After several years and many attempts at rehab, I just couldn't do it anymore. I wanted to die; I wanted to stop hurting and disappointing my family. So I took a bottle of pills and went to sleep. God had other plans for me, but it took a while to get my attention.

I entered another rehab, this time for two months. While I was in rehab I met a man who gave me the attention I so desired. I truly thought I was in love. We got out of rehab about the same time, and my life was consumed with finding a way to be with him. I started drinking again and soon after I was introduced to crack. I turned into someone I hated. All that mattered to me was staying high and being with him. I turned into a thief and a liar, and I broke the hearts of every person I loved. I lost my job, my home, my car, and most importantly, my family. I had a failed marriage and had failed my children, all because of the bad choices that I made and because I tried to fix my life the way I thought it should be fixed.

God finally got my attention; I had had enough. I got on my knees and begged God to take this suffering away from me. I had no money to go to rehab, and I had no one who wanted to help me because I had not followed through on anything else I had tried, so I was on my own. I started looking, and I found Teen Challenge. God made a way, and my parents took me to a Teen Challenge center in East Tennessee. It was a crisis center, a short-term place for me to be off the streets and off the drugs. I was finally sent to Teen Challenge of Mississippi, and my life was changed forever.

When I arrived at Teen Challenge of Mississippi, I was a shell of a person. I had no one and deserved nothing. The staff there showed me the love of Christ; they loved me when no one else did, when I didn't even love myself. I was able to stay at Teen Challenge because of so many wonderful people who donated money so I could have a roof over my head and a place to heal.

I was able to spend 14 months without worrying about how I was going to make ends meet and was able to focus on healing myself. The Teen Challenge team taught me about Jesus, and they showed me Jesus. I had always worked hard, but they taught me how to work for Jesus, to work with a purpose. I learned what healthy relationships look like, and I learned to be accountable and to hold others accountable. They helped me work through so many traumatic events in my life, some of which I had blocked out and didn't even remember. I was no longer numb and had to feel the pain, and once I felt it, I was able to work through it.

I graduated in March 2014, and went back to Memphis. My parents took care of my children while I was gone and were gracious enough to let us stay with them for a few months until I could get back on my feet. I got a job and a car and slowly, God began restoring all the things I had lost. I eventually got an apartment and began rebuilding the relationship with my children.

In May 2015, I met a wonderful, God-loving man. My parents helped us get a house so my kids could finish high school without having to change schools, and we began to build a life together. I now have a successful career, and we eventually got married and have just bought our first home together. We were blessed to have my mentor and true friend from Teen Challenge marry us.

God has restored my life to me, better than I could have imagined. Of course, there are bad days, but now I know whom to turn to when I need help. I have learned to face things head on and to reach out to God for the things I cannot handle on my own. I no longer have the need to escape from myself and my problems; I have a God who loves me and wants the best for me. All I have to do is say His name, Jesus. I have hope, something I've never had before. The chains are gone; I've been set free. My stand on scripture still remains today, Psalm 27:14, *"Wait for the Lord, Be strong and take heart and wait for the Lord."*

CHAPTER 5

From Death to Life
A True Story of a Former Addict Redeemed by the Grace of God
By Lauren Goar

Sitting in the back seat of a Mississippi Department of Corrections vehicle, I was staring at a metal cage between me and the driver; I had tears streaming down my face. The route we were taking was all too familiar; however, the destination was new: Central Mississippi Correctional Facility. In all my years of trouble, this was my first time in a place I couldn't get out of for an extended amount of time. I firmly believe God's timing is perfect. Though I still do not fully understand, I look back over the years and see God's faithfulness in my life and day to day, I choose to trust Him, even when His ways are mysterious to me.

Let me start at the beginning. Come with me on a journey — one from death to life.

I grew up middle-class and came from a divorced home. Both of my parents worked hard, and they also drank alcohol regularly. This reality made drinking alcohol normal to me, even as a teenager. I began smoking cigarettes around 11, stealing smokes from my mom. I was drinking regularly by 15 and began smoking marijuana and using meth by 16. Don't get me wrong; there were normal parts of my life. My parents, at separate times, both coached either me or my sister in softball. In sixth grade I joined the band and began to play the saxophone. Music was my passion, but my drug use and lifestyle choices did eventually take its toll and negatively impacted my life. For instance, I almost did not graduate from high school because of my skipping school and missing too many classes, causing my grades to falter.

I was able to graduate, with honors even. I got into some pretty hot water with my parents that summer. Because of those circumstances, my parents thought it best for me to go to a church camp. I knew, even then, that how I had been living was wrong. I ended up getting baptized that summer, but upon returning home and enrolling in a university, I fell right back into my old ways.

After three semesters I ended up failing out of college, causing me to have to move back home. Unfortunately, I had an affinity for the way meth made me feel, and I liked the wrong crowd. I had a stream of dead-end jobs, relationships, and multiple run-ins with the law. Eventually I became affiliated with a gang. I hurt my family and lost myself. Year after year it seemed I went down the rabbit hole farther and farther. I had lost hope for the future and truly saw no way out.

In 2011, I had been at a new low for several years. This year I met a man who had walked with Jesus before but had backslidden. He and I began going to church. I had quit using meth, but we were still drinking, taking pills, and living together. At one point he got arrested, and I contacted some people we had met at church to see if they could help me help him. The lady I contacted agreed to meet me one day in July 2011. At this meeting we talked a little about my boyfriend, but ultimately, God had other plans. She began to ask about me and my life. For the first time I confessed to someone who I had really become. She led me to rededicate my life to Christ that day, and truly I would never be the same.

I had been trying to get my boyfriend into Teen Challenge, and instead, through all this, I ended up there myself. I was set to go into Teen Challenge of Mississippi for women on a Monday in August 2011. It just so happened the Saturday before I was to leave, I was arrested for a warrant I did not know I had. Apparently I was set up in Hinds County for sales of methamphetamine the year before. While I did not make that Monday intake appointment, after being bonded out of jail, I did eventually arrive at Teen Challenge on August 11, 2011. A month later I was sentenced to 10 years, five suspended and five to serve for a sales charge. I was allowed to stay at Teen Challenge until completion and was told to report to MDOC after I finished the program.

I was so grateful to be at Teen Challenge. It was there I truly surrendered my life to Christ. It wasn't all easy. I woke up some days thinking, "Where in the world am I and how did I get here?" Throughout my stay, God began to reveal Himself to me. I began to read the Bible and enjoy it. We were disciplined and had to learn to face ourselves and the messes we had made. Even though it was painful, there was also this hope that was rising up within me. I was truly becoming a different person. As 1 Corinthians 5:17 says, *I was a new creation!*

In December of that year, the Teen Challenge program moved into a facility in Poplarville, Miss. In April 2012, the program directors resigned, and one of the last things they did was ask me to become an intern, which I had been praying diligently about. I accepted their offer at my eight-month mark, and after I graduated that August, I came back for a one-year internship. I learned to not only become a disciple of Christ; I was learning to be a disciple-maker.

I spent the next three years learning and growing, serving and even learning practical tools for life. The Lord made a way for me to get a car, go back to college, play music again, and also to be a functioning member of society. I learned to pray, and God eventually saved my family, too, over time. At Teen Challenge we spent a lot of time in the Bible, and it was here I learned to stand on the Word of God.

In 2016, I graduated from our local community college with an associate degree, became a youth leader at my local church, and was ultimately let go from Teen Challenge, as God was moving me on. In seeking God's will for what was next, I prayed, like Isaiah, "Here I am Lord; send me; I'll go." I truly meant what I said; I just did not foresee the place He would send me. In 2017, six years after being saved, I was accepted into Bethel School of Supernatural Ministry. I knew I had to get the legal stuff resolved before moving forward. I attempted to do just that, and instead of preparing for school that fall, April 21 of 2017, I was arrested and taken into custody and sent to Central Mississippi Correctional Facility to serve my time. Just like that, my story changed, and again, I would never be the same.

I spent the next 13 months in the Mississippi State Penitentiary. Up to this point, I had been through some trials, but this was the hardest test of my faith to date.

Teen Challenge was a tool the Lord used to prepare me for such a time as this. The challenges and trials of life did not cease because I had gotten saved and sober. Dope was never really my problem — sin was. Sobriety was not the answer — Jesus is.

Today, in 2021, I've since met my husband (whom I had been praying for a long time), had a baby (I did not think I could have children), and am currently employed by a local government office where I am privileged to help others who battle mental instability and/or drug and alcohol addiction, and I help their families as well. Look at God.

I am forever grateful for my time at Teen Challenge of Mississippi for women because it was there I learned to do what I am doing now —- seeking first the Kingdom of God and standing on His promises. My husband I are blessed but are in a trying season even now. Today I'm standing on this promise…

PHILIPPIANS 1:8, says, *That He who began a good work in me will carry it on to completion until the day of Christ Jesus.*

CHAPTER 6

Raised to Life by Jesus Christ

By Rachel Byrd

As long as I can remember, I have suffered from insecurities and rejection. I grew up in a broken home. My grandmother raised me and my older sister; my parents were divorced and involved in drugs and alcohol. I was always looking for something to fill that empty void in my heart.

In high school I would do anything to "fit in," which led me to smoking marijuana and cigarettes. I got pregnant, dropped out of high school, and got married. Soon after I had my kids, my life began to spiral out of control. My pill and meth addiction grew bigger and bigger. At the age of 22, I was charged with my first felony offense for prescription forgery. As the years went on, I got a divorce and lost my relationship with my kids. I was in and out of secular rehabs, in and out of AA and NA groups, multiple detox centers, living from pillar to post with no stability in my life. Sin took over my life, and I had surrounded myself with people in the drug world who could help me support my drug habit. All I wanted to do was to get high.

I was so far gone in my addiction that I could not hold a job, much less provide for my kids. I lived in paranoia daily. I hurt everybody I ever loved and had abandoned my kids. In 2016, I lost my mother to a drug overdose, which rocked my world. We were in our addiction together, but she was my best friend. I had lost several family members to addiction. Several of my family members were addicts — the generational curse of addiction ran wide open in my family all the way back to my grandpa.

I knew no other way except to get my next fix to keep me from being "dope sick." After my mom passed away, my addiction grew worse. I ended up meeting a man I thought was "the one." He was several years older than I, so all I saw was stability. Slowly but surely, he charmed me to nearly kill me. We were so toxic for each other. We did meth together and explored the world together. He became obsessed with me to the point of torturing and stalking me. He became physically violent, and there seemed to be no way out. He was charged with domestic abuse, and I had an order issued against him to protect myself. I now suffer from PTSD from that lifestyle.

In 2018, I was charged with a felony offense for possession of meth and contempt of court. I spent two and a half months in jail. I knew God would stop me and set me down. I knew about Teen Challenge, because my niece went through the program and graduated. Oct. 25, 2018, I entered Teen Challenge, and that was the day my life changed. When I arrived, I was broken from the cruelty of the world. I was lost and hopeless. I could not even hold my head up to look anyone in the eyes.

God used Teen Challenge as a vessel to save my life. As I went through the program, I began to heal from the abuse and trauma that I caused in my own life and allowed others to do to me. It took a while to surrender all to the Lord, but once I did, I found and gained a relationship with Jesus, and my life changed. I have seen the goodness of God all over my life. He has broken the chains of addiction, fear, and anxiety. The more I sought God, the more layers of bondage broke off me.

God has filled that void in my heart that I tried to fill with drugs and men. I was being disciplined at Teen Challenge, although I never knew what that meant. But God…. . He has restored my family, and I have earned my role as a mother again; I am the Godly mom, daughter, sister, and nana I have always wanted to be.

My life is now on the right track. I have two beautiful grandbabies who are my life. I am the intake coordinator for Teen Challenge of Mississippi. When I was offered the promotion, I thought "God, I am not qualified to do these things," but He equipped me to be an assistant to the program director and to help women who were in the same shape I was in.

God has called me to help ladies, and I love watching the transformation in each life that comes through.

CHAPTER 7

Rise Above!

By Ashley Wise

When I heard the knock at the door, I knew it was the police. I grabbed the bag of meth I had left and quietly tried to open the window so I could make a break for it. As soon as I got my upper half of my body out the window, an officer was waiting with a taser in hand, screaming, "Get on the ground!" As I sat there in handcuffs, my face in the dirt, I wondered how my life had gotten to this point. In a ten-year span my pill addiction had grown to an addiction of meth. For seven years solid I used meth by shooting up with a needle daily. I had abandoned my three daughters to be raised by two separate dads. I lived from house to house with all addicts who lived the same way I did. Our goal was to obtain meth daily. We would scheme, manipulate, lie, and steal to get our fix for that day. I eventually began selling meth to support my habit. A guy I dated could get large quantities for cheap, and I knew plenty of addicts who needed it.

Then my addiction spiraled out of control because I had a never-ending supply, but the guy I was seeing got arrested, and my supply was suddenly cut off. Now I had this huge habit and no way to get my fix. So, I began to date drug dealer after drug dealer to keep me supplied with that I needed. Some fellow addicts came up with an idea to break into the house of a man we knew. We could take all the stolen items we got and trade them for cash and meth.

It was not long after this I sat in jail with a felony charge, and my bond was too high to get out. I thought my whole world was over. Looking back, I see that this is what

God used to save my life. In that jail cell I began to have horrible withdrawals, and I feared what my future held. I was tired, just so tired, of the way I was living. I cried out to God in that moment — not to get me out of jail but just to help me. And in that jail cell, a feeling of peace unlike anything I had never experienced before in my life flooded over me.

I began to seek the Lord the two months that I was locked up, but a former drug dealer of mine came and bonded me out. I was getting high that night. Over the next several months, I fell harder into the bondage of addiction. I began using heroin and meth together. I did not show up for my court date and went on the run from the law. I lived in a constant state of fear, anxiety, and paranoia. I had gotten down to 90 pounds. I could feel death right around the corner.

Hours prior to the police capturing me that day, I had picked up my Bible and read it. So going back to the moment I was in handcuffs on the ground, I knew it was the Lord saving me from me. That was the pivotal moment that I surrendered to the Lord. It was a month later I walked into the doors of Teen Challenge. The first few weeks at the program I could barely look anyone in the eyes. I was so consumed with guilt, shame, fear, and anguish. With the help of the Lord, I pressed through, taking it one day at a time. Each day that passed was a little easier. Month after month it was like layers of heaviness and darkness would fall off me as I continued to seek a real relationship with Jesus. He began to restore my mind, body, and soul. We would learn character qualities through work in the classroom that would help guide me. He would bring certain qualities — virtue, pride, discernment, forgiveness, etc. — that I needed to let go of, to gain, or to strengthen.

Eventually I began to see the Lord's goodness poured graciously on my family's life. I got to hold my little girls in my arms after not seeing them or even talking to them for six years. I began to talk to them every week on the phone. Teen Challenge gave me the feeling that the Lord could form me into the woman and mother he created me to be. I began to form this amazingly beautiful relationship with Jesus. Without a real relationship that we grow daily with Him, we have nothing. Now I have a solid foundation to be able to build my life back. I have found true freedom in Jesus Christ. I remember when I was deep in my addiction, the anguish that consumed me, and I compare it to the transformation that I have experienced, and it brings me to tears of joy. The God we serve is so good. I graduated Teen Challenge July 16, 2021. I'm attending a faith-based program that is closer to home in North Mississippi. I do not know all the plans the Lord has for me just yet. But I know that the Lord will be doing the leading as I step out in faith and trust.

Isaiah 61:3 says, *To appoint unto them that mourn in Zion to give unto them beauty for ashes, the oil of joy for mourning, the garment of praise for the spirit of heaviness.*

CHAPTER 8

Dry Bones Come to Life

By Angie Little

Growing up, I always felt like I did not fit in. I had two brothers, two sisters, and a mother who did her best to support five kids. Our dad, suffering from his own addiction, died when I was 11.

When I was 13, I started traveling to Washington state during the summer to visit my sister, and that is when my life changed. I met my first partner and began a 25-year I.V. heroin addiction. At 15, my partner died of an overdose. During this same three-and-a-half-year timeframe, I was sexually abused by my female math teacher. I never felt any anger or hurt toward her. I felt as though I was a willing participant and was unaware it was abuse.

Fast forward to age 18: one of my friends raped me after we got high, and he almost killed me. Not long after that, someone from my father's motorcycle club told me that as payment for the debt my father owed them, my brother and I were to do things for them. So, I did what they said. I have inflicted pain on others and even played God in people's lives at times. This is so hard for me to write because I know that I am not that person anymore. I hate who I was, but by God's grace, I am not in prison, dead, or in hell.

With all that has happened in my life, the hardest thing for me was to forgive myself. I was stuck with what I had become. At 38, I was set free from heroin, and in 2010 my mother became sick. I quit my job of 26 years to care for her because she had dementia. She knew me only as "that boy." When she passed in 2017, I went straight back to the hell I swore I'd never go back to — living in my truck and jumping from place to place, until I ran across this Christian woman I knew as a child.

I was cleaning in her yard one day, and she asked me to help her with her grandchildren. This is when COVID-19 hit. I said I would, so she gave me a room, food to eat, and money here and there, and all I had to do was go to church. Of course, church was limited because of the pandemic, but we still did devotions online every morning. July rolled around, and she asked me to drug test for her before she went on her mission trip, and she wanted me to stay with the kids. I told her I would fail, but she still insisted. I had packed my things while I was waiting for the test results, knowing I was going to get kicked out, and instead, she said something to me that blew my mind. She said, "I'm waiting to see what God would have me do."

A few days later, Teen Challenge of Mississippi, a program that helps women ages 18 and older to overcome addiction of all kinds, contacted me and asked if I wanted help. Since I have been at Teen Challenge, God is restoring my family back to me and has revealed to me that the gay lifestyle I was living is not His will, and that His son's death on the cross wiped away all the bad things I did to others. I now have been forgiven; I have forgiven myself and others. I have been saved. The next step of my life will be to do whatever God will have me to do. I am going to get my G.E.D. and possibly participate in an internship at Teen Challenge to help other women like me. But whatever happens I know I will not keep what has been given to me. I must and will tell the world who my Savior is and what He has done and still is doing for me.

CHAPTER 9

Bound by Anger Set Fee by Jesus Christ

By Randi Jones

For as long as I can remember I have struggled with anger issues. Anger had become my new normal. "I'm so mad" became my catch phrase and was used more than any other combination of words I put together in a day. Do not get me wrong, I had a lot of reasons to be angry, but not only had I let it become the new norm for me; it was also my biggest addiction.

I suffered at the hands of many men and endured all types of abuse, so that was always the first reason I pointed to for fueling my anger fire. Another reason I was angry was that I wanted to be heard. Suffering from sexual abuse, I felt like I had been silenced out of fear that I had been the one to do something wrong. Also, I desired power. I love to be in charge, and anger gave me an excuse to scare people into allowing me to be in control. I loved the way I felt when people feared me. It made me feel important, which led to a false sense of acceptance I had searched for.

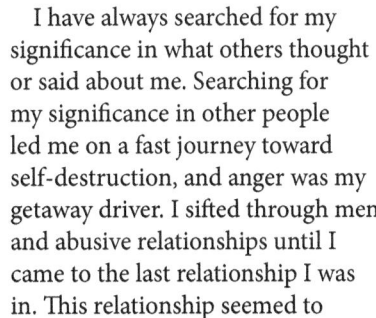

I have always searched for my significance in what others thought or said about me. Searching for my significance in other people led me on a fast journey toward self-destruction, and anger was my getaway driver. I sifted through men and abusive relationships until I came to the last relationship I was in. This relationship seemed to have been the worst of them all, and it went south fast. I thought so highly of this man in my life, I chose him over my own child. I decided to sign my rights as a parent away to my mother and live with this person whom I thought filled the void in my heart. I had no idea I had stepped into a whole new world, and all for the worse.

I noticed him coming to my apartment in an altered state, and he told me he was just taking some pills to chill him out. I had begun to believe the lie that "if he only saw what he looked like on these pills, he would stop. I'll show him." I snorted my first line of heroin, not even knowing what it was. That quickly turned into a heavy addiction. Not long after, I became an IV addict because snorting was not enough. Then I got addicted to crystal meth. We did anything we could to get our hands on anything without getting caught, so we started sharing needles with other users, not even thinking that we were risking spreading disease.

Months went by, and he became sick. He was taken to the hospital and admitted and told me he had to have heart surgery because of his IV use. I hit rock bottom, and by the grace of God, did not die from my own excessive drug use. My pastor sought me out continually, and with God's help, the doors at Teen Challenge opened for me. I am not too sure how the process panned out, but God got me to the center to begin the road to recovery. The Lord has done a miraculous work in me since I walked through those doors. I am a whole new person. I am no longer bound by the chains of anger, or addiction, and now I am on the journey toward helping other women get set free through God's amazing grace. I will never be able to give back to the staff or to Teen Challenge all they have given or done for me, but most of all I will never be able to repay the Lord. He, among many others, has more than enough reasons to have turned his back on me, but instead, he picked me up out of the miry clay and set my feet on solid ground.

CHAPTER 10

Wrong Choices Righted by Redemption

By Jennifer Ford

Mine is a story of wrong choices and God's redemption. Wrong choices and decisions led me down a very destructive path before I ultimately decided that enough was enough and that I needed help from someone greater than me.

When I was 2 years old, my older brother died. Even though I was young, this left a hole in my life that I felt no one else could fill. As I grew up, I began looking for love, protection, significance, and security in guys and male figures in my life. I missed my brother and felt like a piece of my heart was gone.

At 10 years old, I created my own online account, engaging in online relationships with guys I did not know. I think I did this out of jealousy of my older sister. She had a relationship with a guy who lived out of state, and I wanted this, too (even at 10 years old). I very quickly became addicted to looking at pictures of men in ways a 10-year-old never should. This opened the door to a pornography addiction, and I had no idea this was happening. It's amazing how the enemy works to gain control of our minds!

When I was 15 years old, I accepted Jesus Christ as my Savior and Lord. However, at the time, I had no idea what it meant to have a relationship with Jesus. Not long after that, I made the decision to have sex with my boyfriend. Bad decision! That decision caused a great change in me spiritually. I began a downhill descent that would last several years.

I eventually started drinking occasionally (usually on the weekends) with whatever boyfriend I had at the time. I was usually dating older guys because they were old enough to buy the alcohol. I thought it was cool to drink because everyone else my age seemed to be drinking, too.

I continued to drink. I entered college and got a job at Applebee's as a hostess. I met a guy, and things seemed to be great. However, one day, one of my friends informed me that he was married. Even after gaining that knowledge, I continued to see him and sleep with him. I had really allowed Satan to pull me away from Christ.

On July 3, 2012, my dad died. He was my best friend, my hero, my protector. I began to drink more heavily to numb the pain I felt at his loss. I didn't know how else to deal with the pain. I dropped out of college because I could not concentrate because of the pain of losing my dad and my drinking.

A few years later, on June 18, 2014, my pawpaw died. He was my next best friend after my dad. My drinking got worse, but I did return to college, determined to finish. A few months later, my mom had a severe stroke, and my determination to graduate college became even stronger. I found a way to push through, even though I was in tremendous emotional pain.

Shortly after graduating from college, I went to work and was a functional alcoholic. I went to work hungover and smelling of alcohol. I had a severe car wreck that nearly killed me. I was driving drunk and speeding because I was mad at some guy. At this time I was staying wherever someone would let me stay.

To get a fresh start, I moved away from home. That didn't work. I got in touch with a guy I met at a previous job. I was still drinking and had begun to abuse Percocet pills. He and I started dating, and I decided to move back home to be with him. That decision led me to another addiction.

He began being a little abusive, just drinking alcohol. Then he introduced me to Black Mollies. That led me to using crystal meth, Percocets, and morphine pills, along with alcohol and whatever else he could get. The abuse also got worse. He began to toss me around, choke me, slam my head against the wall, shoot a pistol at me, and abuse me sexually. I also saw his young niece and nephew grab him in places they shouldn't. I could see that there was a demonic presence in that house. I prayed several times, while possibly overdosing, for God to let me live and get me out of there.

I finally wrote and sent a letter out to my grandmother. She subsequently got my cousin and several deputies to get me. The day they picked me up is the day they decided I needed more help than they could provide. They got me into Teen Challenge of Mississippi. I arrived there on Oct. 9, 2018.

I persevered and prospered at Teen Challenge and graduated from the program. God really worked in my life through the staff there. He restored my family, my significance, and my identity. I've been freed from all of my addictions. I was baptized and received the Holy Spirit, evidenced by my speaking in tongues. I have learned how to deal with grief His way, not mine. He has taught me how to grieve in healthy ways. I've learned to depend on

God, not man. Man will fall short and disappoint us. God will not. I have learned that revenge isn't mine, it's God's (Romans 12:19). I don't have the desire to engage in any of my former addictions. My mind has been renewed and transformed by Him (Romans 12:2).

Since I've been home, God has blessed me with a wonderful husband and a beautiful stepdaughter. I have started a career working with the state and just got a raise. My husband and I lead Celebrate Recovery at a church close to where we live. My husband has his dream job of working as a firefighter.

God is everlasting, and He is always there, even when you think He isn't. HE IS!! I know what He can do because I have seen Him work in my life. He can do it for you, too! Just yield to His Spirit and leading in your life. He can work miracles if you will let Him.

GOD IS MY REDEEMER AND MY SALVATION!!

CHAPTER 11

Let Freedom Ring

By Shannon Boose

On July 4, 2007, I lay there on that cold, concrete floor in stripes, gritting my teeth and clenching my fists, begging God to help me. He reminded me that I prayed for this. I had prayed a week prior to this day asking Him to help me get out of the dope game, to help me not have to live day by day hustling to get my next fix. I wondered how I let it get that far. I had not seen my three children in two years. It seemed like it had only been a few days. Not only had I abandoned my children, but I had also burned every bridge with my family. I lost all my belongings and now my freedom. How could I have let this happen? This was not me. I came from a good family. I was smart and educated. I had a lot of potential. I was a good mom. I had morals.

However, all those qualities were obsolete after going down the road of addiction. Not long after I fell victim, I fell out of touch with who I was. During this downward journey, I walked out on my children, sold drugs, and lied to myself and others. You may ask why? How?

Genesis 1:1 says, "In the beginning God created the Heavens and the Earth." I feel that this truth is important to my life because my being has been affected in the spiritual realm as well as the earthly realm. Even before I was born, my feelings and perception of life were being formed. Studies say that a child in its mother's womb knows whether it is wanted, accepted, or appreciated. My parents had been married for three years when I was conceived. Their

union was not under God's Holy matrimony, so I believe that my soul was not protected from the lies of self-worth. My mother's pregnancy was not planned, and I was a new challenge in their lives.

My parents got a divorce when I was 18 months old. My mother had custody of me. She worked on the road, and we constantly moved around to different places. Once I started school, I moved in with my grandparents, and my mother would visit me on the weekends and holidays. One of my clearest childhood memories is of my grandmother telling me that my mother was not going to be able to come see me that weekend. I can visualize myself standing in the hallway at my grandmother's house, looking into my mom's room, crying uncontrollably and physically hurting from the feelings of abandonment and rejection. I thought that if she could not come see me, then I was not worth much.

My dad was in and out of my life. I would visit him on holidays and special occasions. I was told that he was sick a lot so I could not stay with him that much. I eventually found out that his sickness was addiction and alcoholism. So many times, he made promises to come get me and never did. I did not understand why he chose drugs and alcohol over me. Once again, the rejection and abandonment gave me feelings of no self-worth.

Throughout my childhood I lived with different family members. There were a few times when my mom would settle into a home but eventually used the excuse that she needed to go to work on the road to make money to pay bills. I lived with my dad when he would get clean and sober, but that never lasted. I had very little stability and structure, and this caused a lot of confusion.

My maternal grandparents were my main role models. They played a big part in teaching me about life. They took me to church and taught me the difference between right and wrong. Even though I was learning about the Bible and scriptures, I perceived that the people in the Bible were perfect people. I believed that if you did something wrong, you were a bad person. I thought that I had to act right to be a good person in God's eyes and to please Him. I thought only good people got to go to heaven.

I was verbally reminded that I was the only grandchild who had divorced parents and that my mom worked so hard to support me. I believed that I was a burden and was ashamed for not having a perfect life. However, everyone spoiled me, and I got everything I wanted. The comfort from the material things lasted only for a short while. This hurt me more than it helped me. I had the understanding that money could buy love. I thought more was better, and my parents loved me at a distance.

I began turning my anger inward and stuffing my feelings. This inward anger became depression, and I tried finding comfort in food. I ended up an obese child. In my fifth-grade school year, I suffered bullying because of my weight, glasses, and frizzy hair. This increased my feelings of low self-worth. I also suffered from loneliness. I was an only child and did not feel like I could relate to anyone.

I was introduced to Jesus when I was 12 years old. I was taught that Jesus could save me from going to hell if I asked Him to come into my heart, so I did. I did not understand the commitment of making Him my Lord and living for Him. I asked Him to be my Savior but not my Lord. I still lived life my way. I was also introduced to cigarettes and alcohol around this time. I began hanging around the wrong crowd and searching for the acceptance I always longed for.

At age 13, I thought I found the love of my life and gave up my purity. I got involved in New Age, Gothic, and thought the dark world was cool. I began smoking marijuana when I was 15. Throughout high school, I used just about any drug I could find, including men. I graduated from high school by the grace of God but went into college with a cocaine addiction. After three years of college and pursuing three different degrees, I gave up on school without accomplishing anything.

I had my first child when I was 21. I stopped using cocaine throughout my pregnancy. After my daughter was born, I picked up my cocaine habit again and eventually ended up in a secular drug rehab. I completed the program after 30 days, saying that marijuana was my weakness/my drug of choice and minimizing my cocaine problem. I relapsed the same day I got out.

About a year later, I was really convinced I had found my true love. This love was crack cocaine, and it controlled the next six years of my life. I found myself pregnant and decided to have an abortion. My excuses were that I didn't have time for another baby, and my daughter wouldn't have as much with a new baby around. Three months after my abortion, I became pregnant again. My mom had me court-ordered to Whitfield, the state hospital, but after six weeks of treatment, I got kicked out and went right back to the party life.

When my son was six months old and my daughter was 3 years old, the Department of Human Services took custody of my children. I could not understand how someone could take babies away from their mother. They were being fed, clothed, and had a lot of toys. I did not consider the emotional abuse and neglect of time that I didn't spend with them. The shame of not being a good mother drove me deeper in my addiction. I continued in my mess for a while and eventually went to the secular rehab, Harbor House, to work on regaining custody of my children. I told them what they wanted to hear, shared my story, did my homework, read the books, and agreed even when I did not agree. I completed the program and proved myself for a while. I got to visit my children, and the restoration process began. But then it happened. I was still carrying the shame and low self-worth, so I went searching again for an answer. I went back to the same old people, places, and things. My children stayed in the same foster home.

This time I basically was on my own. My family had stopped supporting me financially. I began making money to support my crack habit and my living expenses by selling drugs and my body. I ended up pregnant for the fourth time, and a reminder of what a worthless mother I was came back to haunt me. I decided to try to make things right once more. I went back to the Harbor House a second time, more determined than the first. I put a little more effort and sincerity into my recovery. I was sure to make it work this time. I got closer to God than ever before. I completed my fourth rehabilitation program. I had dealt with a lot of my issues but still had low self-worth. It did not take long for me to go back to my old friends. I was searching for someone or something to take away my shame and give me purpose.

I asked my mom to babysit my three children while I went out for a break one night in September 2005. I never came home that night and ran on a binge for two years. My family could not find me, and they did not want to by this time. I was too ashamed to face them for all the pain I had caused. They lost all the respect they had for me. I wondered if I would ever see my kids again.

At first, I was making good money and had all the worldly things I wanted. It was fun and games until I eventually lost my cars, homes, and all my belongings. I would stay up for three and four days at a time and sleep for days at a time. I was living in hotels and struggling each day to pay for rent, food, cigarettes, and my fix. There were days that I did not want to get out of the bed. I wanted to die, but I did not want to kill myself. I would cry out for God to help me.

Not long after I had sincerely cried out in desperation, I was picked up by the police for a secret indictment. I had sold drugs to an undercover police officer. My bond was too high for me to get out of jail, and I realized that it was God's way of answering my cry.

The night that I was incarcerated and lying on that cold, concrete floor, I prayed, "God, if anyone can help me, You can. Do for me what I cannot do for myself. I want to be as close to You as possible. I want to surrender totally to You."

I also prayed and asked God to help me stop smoking cigarettes. Even though the jail I was in was a smoke-free facility, cigarettes still got in there. Every time I was offered a cigarette, I would reject it and say "Lord, I'm doing my part in not smoking, now You've got to do Your part in delivering the taste out of my mouth."

After I spent four months in pure hell, God used my grandparents to intervene and to talk to a judge to have me court ordered to a faith-based program called Teen Challenge. While I was in the Teen Challenge ministry, I participated in Bible studies that worked on the different issues in my life. I studied God's Word, listened to godly counsel, and went to the altar every chance that I got to be touched by God. God delivered me from drugs, cigarettes, and depression. I began to learn the truth about self-worth and my purpose in life. I no longer blamed my parents for not being who I thought they should have been and for the life that was dealt to me. God has helped me to forgive and have compassion for them. Now I realize they did the best they knew how to do, just like I managed the best I knew how. I started taking responsibility for my own actions. I realized that Jesus is either Lord of all or not Lord at all.

My children were still in the same foster home. This foster home wanted to adopt them, and I argued with God that it wasn't fair. For days, I got on my face crying and praying for His perfect will. He reminded me of the story of Abraham and how Abraham had faith and completely surrendered. I finally came to a place in my heart to accept that it was best for my children to be with that family. I was waiting on the adoption papers to come in the mail for me to sign. However, God had other plans. I received a call that they were being placed in the Tupelo Children's Mansion until I could get us a home. We began the restoration process again, but this time it was different. I was being healed and delivered from my choices, and they were in a place where they could be healed, too. I told my children that I was at Jesus school just like they were at Jesus school.

I graduated from Teen Challenge after one year. Not long after my graduation, I had to go to court to face my drug-sale charge. They had postponed my court date since I had been in treatment. I was found guilty and was given a 20-year suspended sentence, five years of probation, and the minimum fine with a fourth of it suspended. My monthly probation fee was waived. God's favor was with me!

I continued to stay with the Teen Challenge ministry as an emerging leader for a second year and became staff a third year. God used the Teen Challenge ministry to help disciple and transform my thinking and beliefs. I had believed that it was too late to become a good mom. I had believed that my family would never love or trust me again. I had believed that I could never be pure again. I had believed that I had no self-worth. But now I had learned that I was a child of God!

I moved back to Tupelo after long prayers and consideration about going back to my old stomping grounds. The Tupelo Children's Mansion recommended that my children should come home one at a time. My oldest daughter, Kaylee, came first. Then my son, Kage, and my youngest daughter, Kadance. God has created a bond between us, despite our separation. The Lord has broken generational curses and has kept them from the bondage of addiction.

I knew that I would need to stay plugged in to God's kingdom so I would not fall off the right track. I began taking classes at Christian Women's Job Corps, and they assigned me a mentor. The classes prepared me to get back into the real world, get a job, and build my confidence. After completing these classes, I was given the opportunity to be the ministry assistant at Christian Women's Job Corps. The next two years God continued to disciple me through this ministry. Once this season ended, I went back to college for radiologic technology. I completed my prerequisites and applied for the radiology program. Out of 118 applications, I was chosen as one of the top 24-point recipients. I was called in for an interview but found out that my felony hindered me from being able to practice in the clinical classes. At first,

I was discouraged, but God has reminded me that some doors are shut for a reason. I believe that journey helped to build my confidence in knowing that I can accomplish whatever He has called me to do. God has showed me that it is not always about the destination but the journey.

A verse that has had a great impact on my life is 1 Peter 3:4. It says, "Instead it should be that of your inner self. The unfading beauty of a gentle and quiet spirit, which is of great worth in God's sight." I thought that material things made me. I wanted outfits with matching jewelry, purses, and shoes. I thought more was better. God is teaching me to be beautiful on the inside. I once was raging on the inside but now I can be comfortable in my own skin.

God has given me a peace and a supernatural high. He has given me purpose. He accepts me no matter what I have done and for who I am. He gives me clarity in place of the confusion from my childhood. He has restored the relationships with my family. He has given me punctuality in place of laziness. He gave me an old job back that I had walked out on. He has freed me physically, mentally, emotionally, and spiritually. He protected my children. He has healed my body from scars and the abuse of drugs. He kept me alive when I would fall asleep at the wheel and when bullets were meant for me. He made a way for me to get off probation after two and a half years and for my felony record to be expunged! He healed me from the shame and pain of my abortion.

Since I have left Teen Challenge, I have continued to seek God's face in several different Bible studies, conferences, churches, and volunteer opportunities. I have learned that I receive more when I give my time and energy to help others. My heart longs to minister to others who are struggling with the same things I have dealt with. God has healed, delivered, and transformed me into a new creation. I know that God has called me, and He has showed me that my purpose in life is to give back what I have received. He has given me a true life, and I want to help others find the true-life giver. I am currently enrolled at Liberty University to get my Bachelor of Science degree in Interdisciplinary Studies. My goal is to be a counselor so I can encourage and give hope to those who are hurting.

I recently got married to my high school sweetheart, Brad. We started dating in high school, lived the party life together off and on for years, and then went our separate ways. He is the father of my two younger children. After years of prayer, God proved His faithfulness to us. We give Him all the glory for bringing us both full circle. We now serve the Lord together.

Isaiah 40:1-2 says, *"Comfort, oh comfort my people, says your God. Speak softly and tenderly to Jerusalem, but also make it very clear that she has served her sentence, that her sin is taken care of — forgiven! She's been punished enough and more than enough, and now it's over and done with."*

God has promised me that my suffering is over. He motivates me to get out of bed every day and be responsible. He helps me be the mother He created me to be. He has given me life. He has taken away my shame and given me self-worth!

CHAPTER 12

From Broken to Conqueror

By Brittany Meeks

Completely broken from the consequences of sin, I entered Teen Challenge in 2007 at age 18. My father is an addict who filled our home with broken promises, turmoil, and eventually complete abandonment. I was also the victim of childhood sexual abuse and rape. My mother and I moved in with my grandparents after losing our home, and within a few months I found my grandmother dead in her bed. This was the last straw for me. I was shattered mentally, physically, and spiritually.

Though my mother raised me in church, my anger toward God caused me, from ages 13 to 18, to run to drugs and a lifestyle of destruction. I was in and out of rehabs and juvenile detention. I was pregnant as a teenager, was kicked out of school and once had my stomach pumped because I'd taken an overdose. After I'd lived through two years of demonic attack with no relief, God spoke to me: "Choose between life or death/"

My mother had very little money to offer, but I was accepted into Teen Challenge (because of others' donations, my life was saved). In Teen Challenge, I developed a love relationship with Jesus that would radically transform my life!

In Teen Challenge God prepared me for every battle I'd ever face. After I graduated, my son was diagnosed with autism. Through the years we have faced multiple suspensions, secondary schools, hospitalizations, and uncontrollable meltdowns. Through every trial God has kept me faithfully and unconditionally

serving Him. God has used me to preach, testify, and lead worship in local rehabs, jails, and churches.

God has blessed me with a godly husband who has raised my autistic son. I've earned my GED and two college degrees. Currently I'm working as a registered nurse on the front lines of this pandemic. God used Teen Challenge to save my life; now I pray that God will use my life to help others.

Acts 20:24 says, *"But my life is worth nothing to me unless I use it for finishing the work assigned me by the Lord Jesus — the work of telling others the Good News about the wonderful grace of God."*

CHAPTER 13

You're Not Good Enough – The Lie I Believed

By Hannah Singletary

What happened? What caused you to go off to the deep end? The answer is quite simple, but the effects of what caused my life to spiral out of control would impact everyone who crossed my path of self-destruction.

My out-of-control life began with four small words that would dictate my every move for the next two decades: You're not good enough.

My childhood was quite normal and noneventful. I had God-fearing parents who loved me and poured into me everything that they had. I wanted for nothing and lacked nothing. To an outsider it appeared that my family was fantastic. My parents tried to nurture my strong will and channel it in the right direction. My mother used to tell me that I would be the perfect child if she could just duct tape my mouth shut. High school is the first time that I can recall feeling not good enough. I always felt like an outsider. Something was different about me, but I did not know what it was, and I did not know how to control my emotions.

As I went through my high school years, I struggled with self-image, and I experienced rejection for the first time. The rejection only fueled my feelings about not being good enough. I would come home from school and would think that if only I were prettier and smarter, if only I could be more, then I would not have to feel the pain of not being wanted.

I jumped from group to group of friends, always trying to figure out who I was and where I fit in. I learned to be a chameleon and adapt to my surroundings. I could be in a room full of people and feel all alone. I struggled with perfection, which I later learned was a coping mechanism to make me falsely feel in control when I felt that every part of my life was not in my control.

It was the night before my 15th birthday when I decided to take that first drink. I will never forget the feeling it gave me — a sense of belonging that I had searched for. I fit in, and I was part of something. People thought I was funny, and they enjoyed being around me. I could be myself. This was what I was missing. I drank that night until I passed out and threw up. The next day I felt awful, but the only thing I could think about was how much fun it was and that I'd I finally felt accepted. Little did I know that alcohol would destroy who I was and almost take my life.

Then came college, which presented a whole new world of opportunity to party. I believe that I came to be a functioning alcoholic during my college years. When I drank, I drank to get wasted. I never understood people who would go out and have one drink and go home. I drank until I passed out or decided to go get some type of drug so I could party even longer. The more I drank, the more I felt like I belonged. I could be myself, I thought.

College ended, and everyone's party stopped — except for mine. I had just gotten married, and I had landed a great job. One would think that this would make me feel complete, but it did not. I still was plagued by the words you are not good enough. I lashed out at everyone around me, blaming them for my unhappiness. I was bitter and full of resentment, but why? I hated myself and everything I stood for, but I thought it was everyone else's fault and that I was just a victim of my surroundings.

I moved to different cities and then I moved to other states, but everywhere I went, there I was. From the ages of 25 to 32, I would experience great loss. I went through a divorce, and within the same year I would bury my mother. Before my mom died, she told me that she knew that one day I'd be okay. "You will be happy and healthy," she said. She fervently prayed for me and believed that God would heal me. Her prayer was that God would bring me to my knees, strip me of every worldly possession, and save my soul.

I was angry that my own mother would pray like this, but little did I know that this prayer would save my life. I got pregnant with my daughter in 2012, which was also the year I had landed myself in rehab twice -- once before I found out I was pregnant and once shortly after. Kensley was born in January 2013, and my binge drinking began a few weeks later. Her dad took her from me and told me to get help. I could not get sober and didn't even know how to try. It was all I thought about. My love for the bottle was greater than the love I had for my child.

It's still hard for me to fathom that alcohol had this kind of control over my life, but it did. I went to treatment for solid year. I saw Kensley only every other weekend, but I was determined to finish the program so I could go home and be a real mom. I stayed sober, if you can call it that, for a few years. I was still miserable, but coherent. Nothing had changed; I still had an ugly heart.

During this time, I got pregnant with my second child. He was my little boy and my second chance at being a mom and doing it right from the get-go. I poured everything that I had into him, and he became the center point for my very existence. I was a super mom, but as you all know, you can't maintain the status of a superhero. I had seemed to get my life together, but there were still those inside issues that I refused to deal with because I could not see past my own nose. I had cleaned up the outside and appeared to have it all together. I had both of my kids, a great job, a new house, and a new car, but I still felt like I was not good enough.

I would come to learn years later that I did not have a drinking problem; I had a heart problem. Getting sober is an inside job. I could not do it alone, and God saw fit to answer my mother's prayer. He took off the gloves and fought all of hell to save my soul.

Kensley was 4 and Tristan was 2 when I picked the bottle back up. It was worse than it had ever been before. They say addiction lies and waits in the dark and grows stronger. My alcoholism took my life to places I never thought I could go. I do not really remember the last two weeks of my drinking. I drank from the time my feet hit the floor until I passed out. The process repeated itself day in and day out. My kids were gone; I had no one, and I felt that I had no reason to live. I thought my kids would be better off without me.

I had a bottle of pills, and I decided to end my life. I had given up. I did not see a way out, but God had a different plan. The following series of events led to my being committed to a psych ward: One day my family could not get in touch with me, so they sent my ex-husband to check on me. I had fallen and hit the bathroom counter. My face was black and blue; my front tooth had been knocked out, and my lip was split from the inside out. Scariest part of all of this was I did not remember a thing. Later that night was the first attempt I made to take my life. I was rushed to the hospital by ambulance and somehow convinced the doctor that it was a mistake, and he let me go home. Two nights later I would make another attempt, and when I arrived at the hospital, the same doctor was standing beside my bed. He said, "You truly had me convinced that you had made a mistake, yet here we are again. This time you will not get one over on me." The next day I was committed. I went straight from the hospital in scrubs and a pair of tall blue socks that had white rubber soles on them. I will never forget walking into that place and telling them that this was a mistake. I proceeded to tell them to get my attorney on the phone. That nurse leaned over and said, "Ma'am, not even God can get you out of here." I thought to myself, "I have really done it this time." None of my family came to see me. I was all alone. At least I thought I was until one night, lying in that cold, dark cinder block room, God showed up. I prayed and asked why and how I ended up here. And I will never forget the chilling response He gave me: "Because in here, I am all you've got. For I know the plans I have for you; I have called you by name; you are mine."

When my family stopped trying to fix me, God took over and made me new. Over the next eight months I took one day at a time and focused on looking at the real me and prayed for God to change my heart. He said, "This time you are going to know that it is not you. I am going to multiply everything you touch." He changed me from the inside out, and He renewed my mind.

I have been free from the stronghold of addiction for almost four years now. I am now the mother my kids deserve. I once was known as the mother who abandoned her children. I left them looking out the door, asking where Momma was because it was getting dark. My kids never have to ask that question again. They are safe, and they are secure, and they belong to God just as I do. I co-parent with my ex-husband, and I am proud to say that he has become my friend. My kids may come from a broken home, but God has healed both homes. God took what seemed to be impossible and made it possible. My life can get stressful at times, but I always look back and remember the days when I couldn't handle anything, and by the grace of God, I can now handle any situation I am faced with.

CHAPTER 14

Why Would God Allow Me to Hurt Like This if He Loves Me So Much??

By Shelia Patterson

"I don't love you anymore" are the words my husband said to me. We'd had 20 years of marriage and two children. We grew up together; we built a life together. Hearing those five words from his mouth brought my whole world crashing down.

Initially, I dove into my Bible. I prayed; I fasted; I claimed scripture; I submerged myself into spiritual things. Inevitably, the marriage ended after a one-year separation. For the first time in 40 years, I was alone. I was not okay with being alone, so I went through one toxic relationship after another, which only added to the rejection I was feeling.

I was raised in church, but I did not have a relationship with God. I knew who God was. I knew all the Bible stories and the books of the Bible. I could not understand why if God loved me so much, He would not stop the tsunami of grief I was experiencing. The pain from a broken heart was overwhelming, and I was sinking deeper and deeper into hopelessness.

What started as drinks after work with my co-workers quickly got out of hand. After leaving my friends I would stop and buy more alcohol. Over the course of about six years, I lost everything I had worked so hard for. I lost my job as a nurse and subsequently my nursing license. I lost my home, my car, and I lost something that could not easily be replaced. I lost the trust and respect of my children, family, and friends.

One by one, my friends said, "I can't stand by and watch you do this to yourself." My family confronted me about my alcohol abuse, but to no avail. My heart physically hurt, and I could not understand why a God who loved me so much would allow me to hurt like this.

On April 2014, I was admitted to the hospital; the amount of alcohol I had consumed had taken its toll on my body, and I could no longer function. It was then I made the decision to go to Teen Challenge. Even though it was the best decision I had ever made, it was hard — Teen Challenge is not for wimps.

In the past seven years, God has done a work in my life that can be described only as a miracle. For over a decade I had numbed the disappointment in my life with medication and/or alcohol. At Teen Challenge I was forced to face all the disappointment and take responsibility for the wrong decisions I had made.

Slowly but surely, God put my life back together again — much like a jigsaw puzzle — one piece at a time. I surrendered my ticket for the emotional roller coaster that I was riding, I gave up the victim mentality that I had held onto for so long and threw away the emotional and mental baggage that I had allowed to weigh me down.

I will be the first to admit that there were some hard days. I had been bound by depression for so long that I could not envision my life without being depressed. I remember telling my mom, "I want to go to heaven because there are no tears there." It took a lot of work — a whole lot —- to finally break free from decades of depression and defeat and lies that the enemy had told me — lies like "nobody loves you; your family would be better off if you were not alive; you're such an embarrassment; you cannot survive without medication for depression and anxiety; God is mad at you."

It has been more than seven years since alcohol has touched my lips! God has given me beauty for ashes. I have the respect and trust of my children and family. God has surrounded me with Godly men and women who love me, pray for me, encourage me, and call me to a closer relationship with God.

I am convinced that the prayers from my family and loved ones are the reason I am alive today. My mother prayed and fasted for me. She claimed scripture over me: Proverbs 22:6 says, "Train up a child in the way he should go and when he is old, he will not depart from it."

When the enemy comes at me, I quote scripture like these:
Genesis 50:20: "You intended to harm me, but God intended it for good to accomplish what is now being done, the saving of many lives."
Exodus 14:14: "The Lord will fight for you; you need only to be still."
Joel 2:25: "... and I will restore to you the years that the locust hath eaten, the cankerworm, and the caterpillar and the palmerworm, my great army which I sent against you."

No doubt, God is the source, and Teen Challenge is the vessel He chose to save my life. Today I am the program director of Adult & Teen Challenge of Mississippi. I also am the ministry coordinator, and I have the privilege of watching God transform these broken, hopeless women into ladies full of the joy of the Lord. I have a relationship with Jesus that could be possible only because of the pain and disappointment I faced, and I look forward to the next thing God is going to do in my life.

CHAPTER 15

From Overdose to Overcomer

By Holley Henderson

I was a high school cheerleader and loved every minute of the competitive side of cheer. During my senior year of high school, though, things took a disastrous turn. While performing a cheer stunt that did not go as planned, I fell and sustained an injury that became the "pain in my neck." Before I turned 20, I found myself in and out of doctors' offices and pharmacies for pain relief, not realizing that by trying to manage my pain, I was building up an addiction to medicine that became my lifeline.

At the age of 22, I was a functioning drug addict. My first year of college I lost my grandmother. After losing her, I did not know how to properly grieve. I found myself filling the void with more prescriptions. On top of the pain pills, I incorporated benzos to help with the depression. I remember walking out of a pharmacy with a big brown paper bag full of controlled drugs. In my prime time, there were hardly any rules and regulations; I am pretty sure that I am one of the reasons the regulations to get pain prescriptions are now so strict. The lifestyle of the drug world became an addiction for me as well. Doctor hopping, selling drugs, transporting drugs, and hiding from the law became a high like no other. It is cliche' but true that one must change his or her lifestyle to get and stay sober.

After college I struggled for a while but soon realized that it was time to grow up, time to get a real job, start a family, and leave the party days in my past. And that I did — for a few years, at least. I got a big-girl job, snagged a husband, and had a beautiful baby boy. Looking back, I honestly think after I had my little boy I was struggling with post-partum depression. He was not even a year old, and before I knew it, I was back in the doctor's office begging for relief. Not long afterward, I started going downhill and went down quick, very quick. They say when you relapse, you relapse harder and faster each time.

Here I am a mother, an accountant, a wife, a daughter, and a friend who was starting to struggle with not only prescription drugs but also now incorporating marijuana and alcohol. The more pressure that was put on me at work and the long nights of walking around the house trying to feed or get my 1-year-old to sleep, the more drugs I was chasing with alcohol and smoking marijuana. It did not take long before everyone around me started noticing I was losing control.

Very soon I lost my job, my husband, and my baby boy. I was in a very lonely and dark place. I was embarrassed and ashamed of not taking care of myself. So many things were going through my mind, and the only way I knew how to cope was to take more drugs.

I remember all too well: It was a Monday night, and I was at rock bottom. I had not been sleeping much or eating and was delirious. I remember getting in my car and leaving. I was trying to escape myself. I remember seeing the blue lights of a police car and knew I was headed to jail. I am not even sure how much drugs were already in my system, but when I saw those blue lights, I immediately turned up the pill bottle and consumed the rest of the variety of pills I had on me. Somehow, I remember being in the back of that police car and trying to tell the cops that I took all the drugs I had. I vaguely remember them getting me out of the back of the police car and into an ambulance. When I awoke, I was in the ICU hooked up to all kinds of monitors, on suicide watch, and had two women from Teen Challenge sitting at the end of my bed. I knew then that my lifestyle almost killed me, but for some reason I was given another chance.

Make no mistake, I was still very hardheaded at this point, and I thought I could help myself as I normally would do. I was not about to give up a year of my life to go to some rehab. Three weeks later, I walked in the doors of Teen Challenge, scared, helpless, hurt, and hoping to find some of whatever it was that helped the two women who were sitting on my bed when I woke up in ICU. I was broken yet rebellious. It took me probably six months after I arrived at Teen Challenge to give it all to God. I spent the first six months of my Teen Challenge journey trying to fix it all by myself. Once I got tired and gave it all to God, my heart started to heal, and I started to change from the inside out.

I am now celebrating my sober date year after year. This date means so much more than just my first day without drugs. This day was the day my testimony started to form. This was the day I decided that I could not do this alone. This was the first day I stopped trying to fix me and reached out for help. It was the day I felt in my heart that I truly wanted to embrace my second chance at life.

Thanks to the grace of God and Teen Challenge for being the vessel to my salvation, I now have the beautiful life that I was destined to have. I regained everything I lost and more. I OVERCAME!

CHAPTER 16

From Rejected to Accepted

By Beth Burgess

When I was 7 years old, my world was turned upside down. My parents divorced, and that same year, we lost our home to a fire. After the divorce, my mom started using drugs and partying, and my dad became an alcoholic. I never knew where I would be staying from day to day.

Once my grandparents realized what was going on, they took me to live with them. I was blessed with wonderful grandparents who raised me in church and loved me like their own. I lived with my grandparents until I was 14, then went to live with my dad and sister. I graduated from high school, got engaged to the love of my life, and got married a year later.

At the age of 22, I gave birth to our son, who is now 17. Six years later, we had our daughter, who is now 11, and our little family was complete.

But then the bottom fell out. On April 20, 2010, I received the worst phone call of my life. There had been an explosion on the drilling rig that my husband was working on. No one could give me any details, so I didn't know if my husband was dead or alive. Thankfully, he walked off that rig without a scratch, but I was so nervous about his returning to work offshore that I got shingles and was prescribed pain medication. This is when my addiction to pain pills began.

I hid my addiction from my husband and family for a very long time. I was a functioning drug addict. I still worked and took care of my family as usual, but my husband started noticing that money was missing, and he confronted me. I came clean about my addiction and went to a detox facility for five days, thinking that after I detoxed, I would be able to go home and stay sober without further treatment.

That was not the case; I ended up using again. This time I accidentally overdosed, causing my kidneys to fail. I was the sickest I had ever been in my life. I told the Lord that if He brought me out of this this time, I would never take pills again. God being the God that He is restored function back to my kidneys. I knew I needed help but did not want to leave my children and husband to do inpatient treatment.

I decided to do outpatient treatment that was not faith-based for 90 days. I completed that program and stayed sober for a little while. But I was still searching for something that would take away all my guilt and shame. So once again I turned back to drugs. I finally decided that I would go to an inpatient facility for 90 days.

My husband took me and dropped me off, and five days later I found myself walking out with only what I had on my back. My husband refused to come get me, so I called my mom to come pick me up. My husband would not allow me to come back home. He said that I had to find another rehab to go to. I found another 90-day inpatient faith-based program that I attended and completed. After being home for quite some time, I started making little compromises, and I relapsed, and this time was even worse. I started using crack cocaine and was in complete darkness. I left our home and was living in motels and didn't know where my next meal would come from or if I would have anywhere to sleep. I was at my lowest. I never thought that I would allow anything to control me the way that this drug did.

I spent all my days chasing my next high. I was finally at rock bottom. At this point my husband didn't know what else to do to help me. He served me with divorce papers, and the only way that I would be able to see my children was for me to go get help again. I made the decision to go to Teen Challenge of Mississippi, a program that helps women ages 18 and older to overcome addiction of all kinds. A friend had completed that program, and I had seen such a big change in her life.

On January 5, 2016, I walked through the doors of Teen Challenge a very broken, angry woman. I was so full of hurt and unforgiveness from my childhood that I didn't even realize was there. I was so angry at myself for becoming a drug addict, something that I had always told myself that I wouldn't be because I didn't want to turn out like my mom.

After being at Teen Challenge for a few days, I knew that was where the Lord wanted me. Teen Challenge was so different from the other rehabs that I had been to. The staff at Teen Challenge were the most loving and Christ-like people I had ever met. They had all been in my shoes, and seeing them walk it out daily gave me hope to do the same.

After watching how these women were allowing the Lord to work in their lives and their families' lives, I decided to rededicate my life to the Lord. I got baptized and allowed the Lord to start working in my life. There was lots of work to be done.

After being at Teen Challenge for six months, I allowed my anger to get the best of me, and I called my mom to come get me. I left Teen Challenge that night, and it didn't take me long to realize that I had made the wrong decision. After talking to my ex-husband, I decided that I needed to go back and let the Lord finish what He had started.

First thing the next morning I called and asked if I could come back. When I arrived back that day, I knew that I had to allow the Lord to start working on my anger, which wasn't an easy process. Once I finally surrendered my life to the Lord and stopped trying to do things my way, my heart started to change. I was finally able to allow the Lord to heal my deepest hurts and started forgiving those who had hurt me.

Once I realized my mom's abandoning me when I was a child was not because of anything I had done, I was able to forgive her and allow the Lord to soften my heart toward her.

While I was at Teen Challenge, my main focus was for the Lord to heal the hurt from my childhood and to restore my marriage. I stayed at Teen Challenge for 15 months and allowed the Lord to change me. On April 1, 2017, I was able to return home to my children and be the mom they deserved.

After I got home and found a job, my goal was for the Lord to restore my marriage. One of the verses I stood on while at Teen Challenge was Job 8:5-6, which says *"But if you pray to God and seek the favor of the Almighty, and if you are pure and live with integrity, He will surely rise up and restore your happy home."*

Slowly, the relationship between my ex-husband and me was restored. On July 24, 2019, my husband and I were remarried. We are now raising our family together. What the enemy intended for harm, God turned around for the good.

CHAPTER 17

You're Never Too Far Gone

By Tina Von Seutter

"It's your fault! I hate you!" These were the words coming from a tiny, hurt, barely 9-year-old girl. She hurled them like fiery darts at her mother as her dad walked out the door and out of their lives. She didn't know it yet, and wouldn't for years to come, but this is the one hurt that would thwart her hopes, dreams, and any chance she might have had to grow into an emotionally secure, productive member of society. It would derail her relationships and eventually her life. See, the thing is, when her Dad left, he also took the mother she knew with him. Mom was there physically, but she was hurt as well. Mom would never really get past the pain inflicted upon her, and as a result, the daughter tried to carry it while burying her own. She learned that to acknowledge something hurt was to acknowledge weakness. So in life, she vowed to be strong and to seek out the higher things: wealth, money, social status, material things. It was all about who you knew and what you had in life. This was her worldview, and she would spend most of her life trying to attain the things of the world to fill the discontentment and emptiness that was her very being.

God? That was something strange people who were too strict and who had no fun believed in. I wasn't going to be one of those people. I was going to live my life. I…I…I…me…me…me. Funny for someone who was a complete fake, not knowing who she was or even liking who she thought she was. No one ever really knew her because she was always who she needed to be in the moment to manipulate whatever situation she was in. Enter alcohol, weed, and eventually prescription pills. The pills were used as a reward system in her household and were "socially acceptable." Now she's entitled and has a superiority complex. When she set her sights on something, she was tenacious. She did have gods, and she lived for them — Motley Crue, Metallica, and on and on and on. She met the right people and went on the road. Her world was filled with coliseums, tour buses, backstage meet-and-greets, alcohol, drugs, parties, tattoos, and sex. These were her gods, and she idolized them. Every relationship she would have after that was measured against these rock stars and lifestyles. They could never live up to that because her version of reality was distorted.

She chose addiction, alcoholism, car wrecks, jail, groupies, marriages, affairs, abortion, divorces, and drugs over children. She made empty promises, lied, manipulated, overdosed, stole, went to rehabs, was both abused and abuser, and hated herself. This was me. That's who I had become. That's all I had to show for the life I lived. I was a broken, hurt woman who ruined my life and the life of anyone I came into contact with.

I love God. That's it. I can look back over my life and see how God had been calling me, sometimes stopping me in my tracks, saving my life and sometimes allowing me to suffer the consequences of my own actions. See, God knew all along it would take my DUI and subsequent Teen Challenge "sentence" to get me to receive His love, to allow Him to transform me, to be a kingdom builder. God knew He had to take away all other options. I had to lose everything and everyone in my life for me to look to Him. God knew who, what, and when. He'd factored it all in. It would be nice if I could tell you I graduated from Teen Challenge and lived happily ever after, but that's not what happened. I now believed in God and knew I needed Jesus as my Savior, but I still wanted to revive things God was trying to kill, mainly, toxic relationships. I still hadn't fully surrendered my life.

So I did what people do in those situations. I slid back into the world rather than working to stay apart from it. My head knew I couldn't be allegiant to both God and the world, but my heart hadn't got the memo. After relapsing, I found myself frail, beat up, alone, and homeless on a park bench. I was self-reliant again, not God-dependent. I was hopeless. Teen Challenge welcomed me back with love rather than judgment. I knew I could have easily died out there. God had saved my life once again, even though I certainly didn't deserve it. Grace. It was in complete surrender, wise counsel, praise and worship, seeking and having a relationship with Christ that my deliverance came, and I knew I'd never be the same. I've heard God audibly once. It was here at Teen Challenge, and He said, "Field of Hope." I didn't understand it at the time. God is good, and His promises do come to pass.

Today, I'm the director of education at Teen Challenge, and I am privileged to see others set free and be a part of their journey. God can change anyone and use anything for His good. He will even use the very things you used to hate about yourself. He turned the tenacity I had once used for evil into a passion to be a witness to His goodness and love. There is hope, and you are never too far gone. All glory to God.

CHAPTER 18

From Death to Beyond Blessed

By Jordan Murphy

I grew up in a Christian home, was raised by my mother and grandparents, and I had a great childhood. But I had abandonment and rejection issues because before I ever met him, my biological father was absent and passed away from an overdose from methadone.

Even though I was raised right, loved unconditionally by my mother and my grandparents, and was brought up in church, I lived off the coattails of my grandparents' faith; I didn't have a relationship with Jesus myself.

I was your typical good kid. I made good grades in school and was really involved in sports. That was my life up until my grandfather passed away my 10th-grade year of high school. I was 16 years old, which is such a critical time in a young girl's life, and it left me devastated. The only father figure I ever had and my biggest fan was gone.

I didn't know how to cope or grieve, so I turned to the approval and attention of boys in high school and of "friends." Peer pressure led to weekend partying, experimenting with weed, pills, and alcohol. Partying became more constant and turned into my seeking a way to feel good. I didn't recognize that I was only trying to avoid facing reality and disappointment.

My senior year of high school I met a guy I thought was everything I wanted, but in the long run, he led me down a destructive path. Midway through my senior year I was introduced to crystal meth. It didn't take much, and I was hooked. This was only the beginning of that long, destructive path.

I did manage to graduate from high school despite all that I had already gotten involved with. One month after graduation, I found myself pregnant with a beautiful baby girl. I sobered up while I was pregnant, but soon after I had my daughter, I relapsed and picked up crystal meth and just about anything else I could get my hands on.

The father of my child and I were still together, and we were using together pretty much every day. We couldn't hold down a job or get our lives together and never could kick the addiction. It only progressed, and our relationship grew toxic and abusive. It was a vicious cycle: The addiction grew stronger, and the abuse just got worse year after year. Mental and emotional abuse turned to physical and sexual abuse. I wanted to leave, but I was so brainwashed and feared that no one would ever love me again.

Year after year in this vicious cycle, the addiction went deeper, and we ended up in trouble with the law, which left us each facing a felony charge. We both ended up on probation, but it still didn't motivate us to get our lives together.

I was given a second chance. I was put on the first offenders' program, but I couldn't get clean to pass my drug test when it was time to report. I failed miserably, so I quit showing up, and everything kept barreling downhill from there.

Still stuck in addiction, we soon lost custody of our beautiful daughter and had to find somewhere to go after being kicked out of my mom's house. We became homeless. Swallowed by addiction and depression, we found shelter in an old, abandoned trailer, which had no running water or electricity. We never knew when we would be able to shower or get our next meal.

At this point, after seven years of being in a toxic, abusive relationship and suffering from addiction, and after being homeless and on the run from the law for six months, I had hit the bottom harder than I ever had before. The father of my child went to jail, and I decided to go home to my family. They gave me an ultimatum: I had two weeks to get out, or I could go to Teen Challenge in Poplarville, Miss.

A few days later, my probation officer was able to contact me for the first time in six months. She told me to come in or she would have to have a warrant issued for my arrest. So, I had to go face her with the possibility of going to prison. I went, and I asked my probation officer if I could be allowed to go to Teen Challenge. She allowed it, showing me mercy that I didn't deserve.

Then came the day that changed my life forever: July 9, 2018. I stepped through the doors of Teen Challenge and committed myself to a yearlong, faith-based discipleship program. I had no idea what the Lord had in store for me.

In November 2019, I completed the program, and I came to know Jesus Christ as my Lord and personal Savior. I learned how to have a relationship and was delivered from religion, addiction, and other strongholds. God restored me and restored my daughter, family, and friends back to me. I have a relationship with my Heavenly Father, and He will never leave nor forsake me.

Since being home from Teen Challenge, I have been living back at home with my family. I'm living as the mother God intended me to be, and He is constantly mending my and my daughter's relationship. My fines have been paid off, and I am currently finishing up the first offenders' program with one year left to go, and once I have completed it, my record will be wiped clean! I have been blessed with a job I have held for almost two years now, and I was recently blessed with the means to get a new vehicle. I'm blessed to also say that I am coming up on three years of being clean and sober, by the grace of God. Sometimes I feel as though I haven't progressed as far as I should have, but then God reminds me where he brought me from, and I know I'm not alone and He is with me every step of the way!

If you ever think you are too far gone, just know that isn't true and you have a Heavenly Father who is waiting on you with open arms. He is always there, no matter where you are, just like His word says in Psalms 139:7-8: *"Where could I go from your spirit? Where could I run and hide from your face?*

If I go up to heaven, you are there! If I go to the realm of the dead, you're there, too!"

There is no place He can't reach you. Let Him give you life because He came to give us life and give it abundantly. Let Him turn your mess into a message and your test into a testimony!

CHAPTER 19

I Found My Voice

By Tiffany Anthony

As I look into the eyes of my granddaughter, I pray that her voice is never silenced. I pray that she never fears to do what is right and never feels ashamed of who she is.

She is 2 years old now. I've known her for less than a year. I wasn't around for her birth, her first words, her first steps, or even her first birthday. I was in jail, unsure of my future. My addiction had finally come to an end, but not by my own doing. It was all God's!

Just days before, I had found myself sitting on the foot of a dirty, cheap motel room bed, asking God to save me from myself and the kind of life I had been living. My choices and habits were slowly destroying me. I had become exactly what I had said I would never be. I felt like a monster, and I hated being in my own skin. He heard my prayers and answered them.

In the middle of the drive to the police department in Laurel, Miss., I ran out of gas after picking up my boyfriend who had been bonded out on a shoplifting charge. That's the moment that God saved me. It wasn't quite like I pictured, but it definitely worked. It was time to start a new chapter in my life. And God gave me the next 15 months to sit down and reconsider my life and what was really important. I also figured out that I had a huge God-shaped hole that nothing else could fill.

It all started when I was 6 years old. A close family member whom I looked up to and trusted stole my innocence. And because of my admiration and the trust I had for this person, I didn't realize that he was doing something bad to me. It was at my babysitter's house that I found out differently. I was saying things to the other children that a 6-year-old should know nothing about. After my sitter discovered what I was saying, she called me into the house by myself. She grabbed me by my shoulders and started violently shaking me. She proceeded to ask me, in a stern voice, "Do you want me to tell your mother what you have been saying?!" I got very scared. I didn't want to get into trouble. So, I promised her that I would never say those kinds of things ever again.

That became the philosophy that Satan etched into me. Never tell anyone anything because in the end I would be in trouble. I never told anyone about any of the bad things that happened to me. I just kept them bottled up inside, eating me alive.

My brother accidentally killed himself just days after I turned 8 years old. He was only 15. The moment he died, my mom stopped "living." She started "existing" only to get me grown. His death sent her mental illness spiraling out of control. When I turned 12, I started searching for any way to escape her illness. I soon became a teenager searching for acceptance, love, and guidance. All I found was attention in all the wrong ways. I didn't know how to cope, and that's when I found drugs, sex, and alcohol. I wanted to numb my reality. I didn't realize that I was walking into Satan's trap.

I got pregnant on purpose at 16 and got married 22 days before I turned 17, just to escape my mom. I got divorced at 19 and met my "Prince Charming." I started attending college at USM and managed his family-owned neighborhood grocery store. I thought that I had everything I could ever want. It was my dream-come-true — until the abuse started.

He eventually put me in the hospital for three days. I had six broken ribs, a collapsed left lung, and a chest tube. Of course, from fear and shame, I lied about what happened. Less than a year later, I found out that I was pregnant. I couldn't take the abuse anymore. So, I packed up my 7-year-old son and never looked back. After getting numerous threats, I decided that the best thing that I could do for my new baby was to allow him to be adopted. My brother's dad and wife adopted my baby. My infant son left the hospital without me. I couldn't and wouldn't allow him to suffer because of my mistakes and bad decisions.

I met a man who was 16 years older than I and fell in love. In fact, he became an idol to me. He wasn't physically abusive, but he was mentally and emotionally abusive. We were together for almost six years when he committed suicide. I turned my recreational drug use into a way to punish myself. I became my own worst enemy. Satan had me, and I couldn't break free.

After my addiction to meth was in full force, I also acquired another addiction — to men. I never allowed myself to get attached, but I couldn't be alone.

Two years after the man I loved died, my mom died. She died alone in Whitfield, a state mental institution. The only person I had left was my son. And that pushed me over the edge. I wasn't much of a mom before losing my mom. I used to pawn him off on her until she had to be hospitalized. After she died, I just completely abandoned him to live with a friend of mine. I was so high for the next eight years that I can barely remember most days, at least until that day sitting on the bed in that motel room, begging God to save me from myself.

God definitely hears prayers. He might not answer them exactly like we want Him to, but He will answer them according to His will. He gave me a chance to sober up, see my fault and my wrongs, ask for forgiveness, get saved, and learn to *"Be still and know that I am God."* (Psalm 46:10)

I was sentenced to Teen Challenge and arrived there June 8, 2020. I was their first intake after the COVID-19 quarantine ended. I was baptized with water on June 15. The women and pastors of Teen Challenge will forever be my family. That's where God sent me to heal and to become a new creation in Christ, to experience the restoration of my family, and where I gained the tools and knowledge needed to defeat Satan and his tactics.

Now I am at The Gap Home. I was accepted back at USM; I volunteer every chance I get; I regularly attend recovery classes and church every Sunday. God is still healing my heart and my body, but every day gets better and better. I can now look into the mirror and not be haunted by my past and all my sins. Now I see a daughter of the one true King, made in His image with a purpose and a plan for the future, and an overcomer by the blood of the Lamb and the word of my testimony.

My heart desires to be a part of jail ministry. I know first-hand how it touches hearts and gives hope. I also have a soft spot for kids. I will be their voice when they can't find their own. I am taking all the bad things that I went through and using them for good. My story isn't over; it's just begun! I found my hope, and his name is Jesus!

A poem I wrote:

What Jesus Had to Say

The devil almost had her, he almost had his way.
But he wasn't counting on what Jesus had to say.
Satan had his grip on her, he had sent addiction in.
But Jesus spoke up and said, "I forgive you of your sin".
All her life, all she knew was loss and every kind of pain.
And every kind of high was just temporary gain.
Just to make the hurt stop and dry up a few tears,
Just to get through another day and forget all her fears.
She felt like a throw away, like she was easy to replace.
She had no idea how much she was really worth —
God's amazing grace.
She thought no one could love her, all her hope was gone.

But God was right beside her, the greatest love ever known.
He was already saving her, she didn't have a clue.
He was already mending her broken pieces with something stronger than glue.
He had sent the Holy Spirit in to wrap her in His arms.
To rescue her from Satan and all his many charms.
Satan tried to destroy her family and pull them apart.
But he wasn't counting on Jesus and the healing of her heart.
So now Satan has to restore all the things he took away.
That's because he wasn't counting on What Jesus Had To Say!

About Adult & Teen Challenge

Adult & Teen Challenge offers faith-based recovery for women struggling with life-controlling problems like drugs and alcohol. Here, Intake Director Rachel Byrd tells us about the nonprofit's past and what's on the horizon.

WHAT IS YOUR ORGANIZATION'S MISSION, AND WHEN AND WHY WAS IT FOUNDED?
David Wilkerson, an Assemblies of God pastor who left a rural Pennsylvania church to work on the street among teenage gang members and socially marginalized people in New York City, founded Adult & Teen Challenge in 1961. He is perhaps best known for authoring "The Cross and the Switchblade" and founding Times Square Church. Adult & Teen Challenge started its first residential program in December 1962 in a house in Brooklyn, N.Y.

In 1973, 12 years after the ministry began, Adult & Teen Challenge established a national headquarters. In 2020, Global Adult & Teen Challenge had established more than 1,400 accommodation centers in 125 countries around the world.

Adult & Teen Challenge in Mississippi has operated successfully for over 35 years. It offers freedom to women 18 years or older from addiction of all kinds — alcoholism, drugs, depression, anxiety, victim mentality, unforgiveness, and many other strongholds that bind women.

Our mission is to provide adults and teens freedom from addiction and other life-controlling issues through Christ-centered solutions. Through effective disciplines, mentoring, and life skills training, ATC and its affiliates have seen positive outcomes and radical life transformation throughout its 60-year history.

Our program lasts 12-18 months, and this time frame provides ample opportunity for adults and teens to confront their destructive choices, self-sabotaging behavior, and unhealthy views. It then gives them a safe place to establish a new "normal" — assured of the love of God and under the guidance of biblical principles. Through our Bible-based curriculum, students learn how to apply God's word to their lives. They also learn to recognize the Holy Spirit's work in their lives, invite God to help them with their life-controlling problems, and become more like Christ.

WHAT IMPACT HAS YOUR ORGANIZATION HAD ON YOUR COMMUNITY?
The impact our ministry has on our community is showing that the Lord can heal the broken and offer evidence of hope. We show the joy of

the Lord and minister all over Mississippi and other states with dramas and powerful testimonies about the transformative power of the Holy Spirit.

WHAT IS THE GREATEST THING YOU HAVE LEARNED OR GAINED BEING PART OF THIS ORGANIZATION?

The greatest thing we have learned or gained is healing, freedom from life-controlling issues, gaining a relationship with Jesus Christ, restoration in families, purpose in life and the reality that God never gives up on us.

WHAT IS SOMETHING ABOUT YOUR ORGANIZATION THAT OTHERS WOULD FIND SURPRISING?

Something about our organization that students would find surprising is the amount of love they are shown. We accept them just as they are, and there is a family atmosphere at our center. It is a ministry that God uses as a vessel to save lives and as a discipleship program.

WHAT'S NEW OR UPCOMING WITH YOUR ORGANIZATION THAT YOU'RE EXCITED TO SHARE?

In 2021, we added a greenhouse and garden center. This not only provides food for our center, but also students are learning life lessons about the importance of tenderness and consistency in growing fruits and vegetables, as well as determination to care for plant life.

We also are excited about the release of this book. We were approached by a local author to share the victories of Teen Challenge graduates and their stories of overcoming a lifetime of addiction and destructive behavior. We partnered with a Gulf Coast publisher who is helping put our stories together and encouraging us to share the truth behind the book's title: "There's Hope Breaking Invisible Chains."

www.ingramcontent.com/pod-product-compliance
Lightning Source LLC
Chambersburg PA
CBHW071230160426
43196CB00012B/2459